The Usborne
STORY
OF
PAINTING

Anthea Peppin

Illustrated by Joseph McEwan

Designed by Graham Round and Kim Blundell

Edited by Robyn Gee

Contents

Anthea Peppin works in the Education
Department of the National Gallery, London.

Consultant Editor: Dr Anne Millard

First published in 1980 by Usborne Publishing Ltd,
20 Garrick Street, London WC2E 9BJ. Copyright © 1980
Usborne Publishing Ltd.

Printed in Belgium

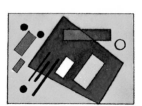

Cave Paintings

No-one knows when the story of painting really began. The earliest paintings that we know about were done about 30,000 years ago, in the Old Stone Age. They are on walls, deep inside caves. People probably painted on other things, such as bark and skin as well, but no evidence for such paintings survives.

We can only guess at why people began to paint pictures, but it seems likely that they did them for magical or religious reasons.

Hunting magic

Most prehistoric cave paintings show large animals such as horses, mammoths and bison, like the one above. Some of the best-preserved and most famous ones are at Altamira in Spain and Lascaux in France.

Most of the paintings are in deep caves. They often show arrows or spears pointing at the animals. It seems likely that they were painted because of hunting magic, rather than to provide decoration.

How cave paintings were done

Brush made of animal hair tied to a small bone

The paint is stored in hollow bones with lumps of fat in the ends

Lamp made by burning fur or moss soaked in animal fat

Grinding coloured rocks between a stone and a bone

In 1940 some very famous cave paintings were found at Lascaux, in France. Some boys were taking their dog for a walk. It disappeared and they eventually found it in the cave.

FRANCE

• Lascaux

• Altamira

SPAIN

Prehistoric people had to make their own paints. They ground up certain coloured earths to make reddish, brown and yellow pigments. They mixed this powder with blood, fat, egg white or plant juice to make a kind of paint, which they put on the walls with brushes made of animal fur or feathers and pads made of moss or leaves.

Egyptian Paintings

1

In Ancient Egypt art was closely linked with religion. The Egyptians believed that when people died they went to live in another world. In order for this to happen the dead body had to be preserved as a mummy. It was dried, wrapped in cloth and put in a painted case.

2

The tombs of dead people were decorated with paintings. These showed the life they had lived on earth, and the kind of life they were expecting in the next world.

4

This tomb painting shows a harvest scene. Important people were always painted larger than their servants and slaves.

3

Special spells written on scrolls in hieroglyphs (picture writing) and illustrated with paintings have been found inside coffins. These are known as the Book of the Dead.

5

Although the remains of the temples and palaces built by the Ancient Egyptians are now mostly bare stone, they, too, were once decorated with paintings.

A different way of drawing

1

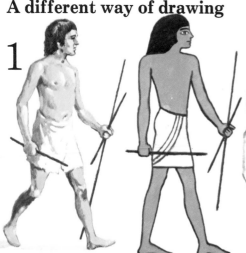

Modern view · Egyptian view

Egyptian painters showed things in a way that seems strange to us. In pictures of the human body, the head, arms and legs were shown from the side but the body and eyes are seen

2

from the front. In the picture above, the ducks, fish and trees are all shown from the side but the pond is shown from above. The things they painted are not very real-looking, but

3

all the parts of the picture they thought important are shown more clearly than you would be able to see them in real life. For them, the purpose was to record things.

Painting in the Ancient World

The art of the Ancient Greeks and Romans is called Classical art. When the Romans took over the Greek Empire they were strongly influenced by Greek sculpture and painting, and the Classical style has continued to influence European artists ever since.

Greek vases

Later vases have red figures on a black background.

Early vases have black figures on a red background.

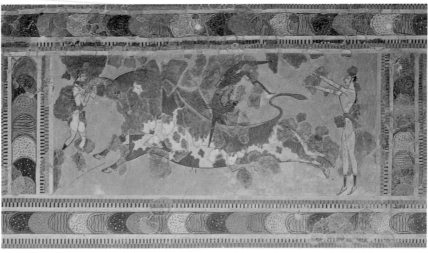

Between 2500BC and 1000BC there were people living on the island of Crete who were very skilled artists.

In the ruins of the palace at Knossos, many wall paintings, like the one above, have been found.

The Etruscans

The Etruscans were the ancient inhabitants of central Italy, who were later conquered by the Romans. They admired Greek art and imported many Greek vases and statues. They also admired and copied Greek painting. Some of their paintings, done on the walls and ceilings of tombs cut into rocks, have survived. This one of musicians dates from about 480BC.

We know from ancient writings that the Ancient Greeks covered their walls with paintings, but most of these have disappeared. Many painted vases have survived, however, and these show us what Greek painting was like. On early vases the figures are rather awkward looking, but on later ones they are more life-like.

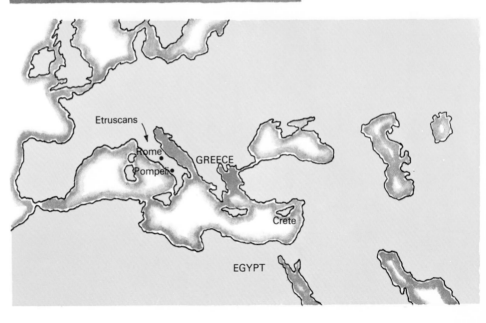

4

Roman paintings

1 When the Romans conquered the Greeks, Roman collectors brought Greek works of art to Rome. These were copied by Roman artists. The copies that survive are mainly statues made of marble and bronze.

2 In AD79 Mount Vesuvius, a volcano in Italy, erupted and buried the town of Pompeii and other nearby towns in hot ash and lava. Many houses and villas in these towns had paintings on their walls.

3 When archaeologists excavated the houses they found that some of these paintings had been preserved.

4 Some Roman wall paintings show graceful figures, like this girl picking flowers.

5 Views of buildings and landscapes made the rooms they were in seem bigger.

6 Portraits painted in the Roman style have been found on Egyptian mummy cases.

Early Christians

The first Christians in the Roman Empire worshipped in secret. In Rome they often used underground tomb passages called catacombs. The pictures found on catacomb walls show people from Bible stories.

The paintings of the early Christian artists are very clear and simple and the people look rather stiff. This is because they were more interested in telling a story than in painting realistically. This picture shows Jesus Christ as the Good Shepherd.

The Middle Ages

In the 4th century AD, Christianity was established as the official religion of the Roman Empire. From this time onwards, the Christian religion had a strong influence on all forms of art.

In the 5th century AD the Roman Empire in the west was overrun by barbarian tribes, and, for a time, art and learning continued only in the monasteries. The eastern (Byzantine) part of the Roman Empire survived and there painting continued as before.

Holy images

Artists in the Byzantine Empire painted pictures of saints and holy people. These are called icons (images). They show unreal figures against gold backgrounds.

In the 8th century a group of people who disapproved of icons gained power. They destroyed all those they could find. They were called iconclasts (image-breakers).

1 Art and learning in the monasteries

Between the 5th and 12th centuries Christian monks were the most important artists in Europe.

Scribe (he copies out the text)

Rubricator (he puts in initial letters and section headings)

Illuminator (he puts in the decoration)

Bound volumes

Mixing paints

Vellum

The room where the monks did their writing was called a scriptorium.

Monks copied out the Bible and other religious books by hand on to a specially fine type of parchment (animal skin) called vellum. Most of the writing was in Latin.

They illuminated the margins, initial letters and sometimes whole pages with pictures and decorations. Illuminating one book may well have taken a monk his whole life.

2

These pages are from the Lindisfarne Gospels, a book made around 700AD by monks on the island of Lindisfarne, off the north of England. The decoration is so elaborate that it

3

probably took the artist several days to complete one square centimetre. On the left is a full-page decoration; on the right a decorated initial (first letter of a new section).

Gold leaf

Gold can be beaten into sheets so thin that you can see through it. It used to be stuck on paintings or illuminated manuscripts. Sometimes it had a pattern pressed into it.

Frescoes

A fresco is a painting done on damp plaster. It dries very quickly so the painter must work fast. Mistakes cannot be corrected. If dry plaster is used the paint will peel off later.

1 Giotto

The Italian artist, Giotto, (AD1267/1337) became famous for doing paintings that looked much more real than other paintings of this time.

2

He was employed to paint wooden altarpieces and frescoes on the walls of churches in Florence (his home town), and several other Italian cities.

3

His frescoes in the Arena Chapel in Padua tell stories from the life of Christ. He tried to show what people were feeling instead of using them as decoration. These people are mourning because Jesus is dead.

4

No shading   Shading

Giotto tried to make his people life-like by using shading to make them look solid.

Pictures in churches

In Western Europe people argued about whether to allow pictures in churches. In the 6th century Pope Gregory the Great declared that paintings were useful for teaching and reminding people about the Bible. After this it became usual to have pictures in churches.

Pictures to stand on the altar were painted on wooden panels. They are often in three sections, like the one above. This is called a triptych.

Originally sculptures, like this one, were often painted in bright colours.

Sculptures carved from stone, showed saints and stories from the Bible.

Stained glass windows often show Bible stories as well as patterns.

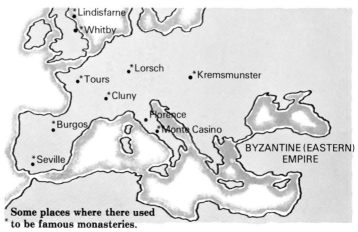

Some places where there used to be famous monasteries.

*Lindisfarne
*Whitby
*Lorsch
*Kremsmunster
*Tours
*Cluny
*Burgos
Florence
*Monte Casino
*Seville

BYZANTINE (EASTERN) EMPIRE

The Early Renaissance

In Italy in the early 15th century, people began to take a great interest in art and learning. Artists started experimenting and asking questions instead of following the style established by tradition. Painters began to paint more and more realistically. They became specially interested in the works of art created in Ancient Greece and Rome, so the time became known as the Renaissance, which means rebirth or revival.

This fresco, by an artist called Masaccio (AD1401/1428) is on the wall of a church in Florence. It shows Christ with his disciples, and St Peter paying the tax collector. Masaccio's figures look solid, every face had its own character and each person has room in which to move. At that time, this way of painting was considered startlingly different.

What is perspective?

For many years artists had realized that to make things appear far away, you have to draw them smaller. In Florence in the 15th century a set of rules was worked out so that this could be done scientifically. We call this system perspective. When it is used to paint people they look much more solid and real, as in Masaccio's painting.

How paints were made

Powdered colours (pigments)

Fresh egg yolk

Pestle and mortar for mixing paint

Water (mixed with egg yolk)

Until recently there were no ready-made paints; painters had to mix their own. In the 15th century Italian painters used a paint called tempera. Here are the ingredients.

Using the ideas of the Ancient World

Italian artists looked at things made by the Greeks and Romans for inspiration. Painted portraits became popular. They were often done in profile (side view) like the portrait heads on Roman coins.

Artists also began to use stories and characters from the myths and history of Ancient Greece and Rome in their paintings. Here are Venus (goddess of love) and Mars (god of war) by the artist Sandro Botticelli (AD1445/1510). Botticelli is probably the most famous painter of the Early Renaissance. Several of his most famous paintings were done for the Medici family.

1 Becoming a painter

To become a painter a boy had to become "apprenticed" to a master in a workshop. There he learned to make paint, clean brushes and palettes and to draw.

After he had served as an apprentice for several years he might become an assistant. He would put in outlines and paint the background and some of the details.

Eventually he might become the master of a workshop. The master did the main bits of the painting. He belonged to a guild which licensed him to sell paintings.

1 Producing a painting

Artists did not just produce any painting they felt like and then hope to sell it to someone. Most paintings were specially commissioned by a noble, a churchman, a merchant or some other wealthy man. The master would probably have gone to see this "patron" to find out what kind of painting he wanted and see where the painting was to hang.

Then the patron had a contract drawn up. This stated the size, subject and price of the painting. Sometimes it also laid down the number of figures and the colours.

Back in the studio the master planned the painting, the apprentices prepared the materials and the assistants started work. The more the patron had agreed to pay, the more painting the master actually did himself. At the end he would check the whole picture to make sure he was satisfied with the standard of work.

A famous patron

This is Lorenzo de Medici, the head of the most important family in Florence during the 15th and 16th centuries. The Medici were famous for their patronage of art, architecture and learning.

Painting in Northern Europe

At the time that the Renaissance was starting in Italy, artists in the north of Europe were painting in a very different way. Their paintings were full of detail and jewel-like colours. Italian ideas spread to the north later.

In the 16th century changes in religious thinking led artists in Northern Europe to produce many more non-religious paintings.

In the 15th century, the cities of Tournai, Ghent and Bruges in Flanders were great centres of the wool trade and of weaving and making tapestries.

This meant that, besides the aristocrats, many people of the merchant class now had money to spend on such luxuries as paintings.

Oil paints

Oil

Pigment (colour)

While Italian artists were still using tempera, artists in Flanders were using oils. Oil paint dries much more slowly, so artists can work more carefully and in much greater detail. It also gives richer colours.

A master of detail

Portraits were popular in Northern Europe. This double one is by Jan van Eyck. Notice all the details he has put into it—the slippers, the fruit, the dog's hair. In the mirror at the back of the room you can see the whole scene reflected from behind.

A painter of nightmares

Many of the paintings by Jerome Bosch are crammed with strange details. This is what he imagined hell to look like.

These are some of the weird and ugly creatures from his painting of hell enlarged so that you can see them more clearly.

Italian ideas spread to Northern Europe

This is the German, Albrecht Dürer, doing a self-portrait. Dürer, had travelled to Italy. He was impressed by Italian ideas and wanted to spread them to other artists.

Making an engraving.

Printing copies.

One way of spreading ideas was to make engravings of paintings and print lots of copies. As well as being a great painter, Dürer was one of the first great engravers.

Dürer was always experimenting with ways of painting things more realistically. Here he is looking at his model through a pane of glass and painting what he sees.

Portraits for a king

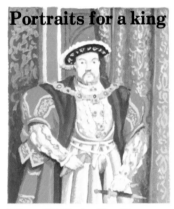

Hans Holbein the Younger (his father was also an artist) was another German who knew about Italian art. He went to England and worked for Henry VIII.

Henry VIII was so impressed by Holbein's paintings that he gave him the official title of court painter. His main job was to paint pictures of the members of the royal household, so most of his paintings are portraits. He also designed jewellery, decorations for halls and costumes for pageants.

Henry was thinking of marrying Ann of Cleves, but he had never met her. He sent Holbein to do this portrait of her, so he could see if she was pretty.

Everyday scenes

Pieter Bruegel, a Flemish painter, is famous for his pictures of everyday life, like this one of children playing. He painted ordinary, often ugly, people at work or enjoying life.

Famous artists

The Netherlands

AD1378/1444	Robert Campin
AD1390/1441	Jan van Eyck
AD1399/1462	Rogier van der Weyden
AD1440/1482	Hugo van der Goes
AD1435/1494	Hans Memling
AD1450/1516	Jerome Bosch
AD1525/1569	Pieter Bruegel

Germany

AD1460/1528	Mathis Grünewald
AD1471/1528	Albrecht Dürer
AD1473/1553	Lucas Cranach (the elder)
AD1489/1538	Albrecht Altdorfer

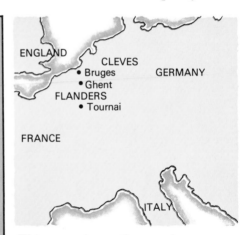

This map shows the area known as Flanders. It was the southern part of the "Netherlands" or "Low Countries" and is roughly the same as modern Belgium and Luxembourg.

The High Renaissance

The period between about AD1500 and about AD1527 in Italy is called the High Renaissance because people feel that this was the time of greatest artistic achievement. Rome replaced Florence as the most important centre for artists, and the Popes became the leading patrons in Italy.

Three artists stood out above all the rest. They were Leonardo da Vinci (AD1452/1519), Michelangelo (AD1475/1564) and Raphael (AD1483/1520).

Mona Lisa

This is Leonardo's most famous painting. It is the portrait of a Florentine lady and is called the Mona Lisa. It is painted in soft colours, as though everything is seen through a slight haze. The blurring of outlines, which gives this effect, is called *sfumato*. The lady's skin glows and the shadows on her face are very soft. The strange landscape behind adds to the air of mystery given by her slight smile. There is a story that Leonardo hired musicians to keep her amused while he painted.

Leonardo da Vinci

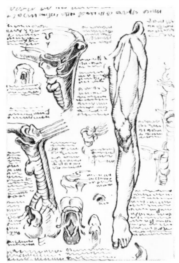

Amazing records of Leonardo's work survive in his notebooks full of sketches and notes written in mirror writing.

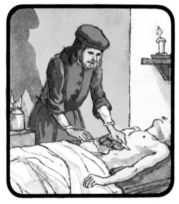

He also studied the human body by cutting up corpses. Eventually the Pope forbade him to do this.

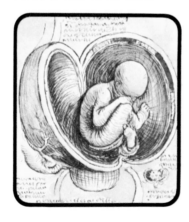

He made sketches of the bodies he cut up. This is a drawing of an unborn baby.

He had many interests besides painting. He studied nature in a way that no one had done before and he was also a most original inventor. Here he is in his room, studying plants and insects that he has collected.

Leonardo was interested in so many things that he did not always finish what he began. He left many unfinished paintings. This is a design or "cartoon" for a painting he never did. It shows the Virgin Mary, Jesus, St Anne and St John the Baptist. Only about 15 finished paintings by him survive.

Michelangelo

Experts now think that Michelangelo was probably standing up, rather than lying down, when he painted the ceiling of the Sistine Chapel.

Michelangelo was a sculptor, an architect and a painter. His best known painting is the fresco on the ceiling of the Sistine Chapel in the Vatican in Rome. On it he showed scenes from the Bible and numerous other figures. It was an enormous work and he did it all by himself. It took him four years to do. He had to work on scaffolding and he found that painting over his head was a great strain.

Raphael

This is a detail from the Sistine Chapel. It shows God creating Adam. The figures almost give the impression of being sculptures.

Plato   Heraclitus

The painter Raphael was in Rome at the same time as Michelangelo. They knew each other but did not get on well together, although they admired each other's work. Raphael was also working for the Pope. He painted some small rooms (known as Stanze) in the Vatican. One of these shows the "School of Athens". In it Raphael has imagined what the Ancient Greek scholars and thinkers would have looked like.

In the "School of Athens" the figure representing the philosopher Plato is thought to be a portrait of Leonardo, while Heraclitus may well be a portrait of Michelangelo.

Late Renaissance and Mannerism

People thought that the art of the High Renaissance was so perfect that it was very difficult for young painters of the next generation to find ways of improving on the past. Some of them reacted by breaking the rules of Renaissance painting, and distorting the figures and space in their pictures. This often looks very dramatic. We call this style Mannerism.

In the 16th century young artists studied hard to learn from Michelangelo's paintings, particularly the ones he did towards the end of his life. These contain lots of nudes in complicated positions, like these ones from his picture of the Last Judgement, painted on the altar wall of the Sistine Chapel.

Some painters chose to exaggerate certain parts of the body to achieve a particular effect. This picture by Parmigianino is called "The Madonna of the Long Neck". Other parts of Mary's body, besides her neck, have been elongated to make her look graceful. Artists also made the space in their pictures look strange. Notice how small the man in the right corner is, and how the angels are crammed together on the other side of the picture.

An early art historian

The artist Giorgio Vasari travelled all over Italy, finding out about artists and works of art. He used this information to write a book about the history of art. It was published in 1550. Much of what we know about early artists comes from this book.

Famous artists

Mannerists

AD1494/1556	Jacopo Pontormo
AD1503/1540	Francesco Parmigianino
AD1503/1572	Agnolo Bronzino
AD1511/1574	Giorgio Vasari

Venetians

AD1430/1516	Giovanni Bellini
AD1478/1510	Giorgione (Giorgio del Castelfranco)
AD1490/1576	Titian (Tiziano Vecellio)
AD1518/1594	Jacopo Tintoretto
AD1528/1588	Paolo Veronese

Painters in Venice

Not all the Italian artists in the later 16th century were Mannerists. In Venice, which was rather isolated and different from the rest of Italy, artists had developed their own style or "school". Venetian artists, like those of the High Renaissance, were specially interested in colour and light.

Most of the famous Venetian artists painted altarpieces. Some of these large canvas paintings are still standing in Venetian churches.

Painting on canvas

At about this time, canvas began to be widely used instead of wooden panels. Canvas has to be stretched and coated with size (a type of glue) before you can paint on it.

Cleaning old paintings

Canvas rots with age, especially if it is allowed to get too damp or too dry. Nowadays picture restorers can preserve old paintings by transferring them to a new piece of canvas.

Friend of kings and emperors

The most brilliant and famous of all the Venetian artists was Titian. All the most important men of his day, from the Pope and Emperor downwards, were eager to have their pictures painted by him. He helped to make full-length portraits fashionable. This portrait of the Emperor Charles V, was done in 1530 and is one of the first of its type. Titian became a personal friend of Charles V, which, in those days, was an unheard of honour for an artist.

Baroque Painting

In the 17th century a style of art known as Baroque developed. It was especially well suited to large scale pictures—the kind of painting you would expect to find in a church or palace. There was most demand for works like this in Roman Catholic countries such as Italy, Flanders and Spain.

Painted ceilings were very fashionable at this time. The artists painted stone structures so cleverly, that from the ground they look real. The figures are also painted as though seen from below and appear to be floating through the air. This effect is known as "illusionism".

Studying ruins in Rome

The paintings of Caravaggio influenced painters all over Europe. He used strong contrasts of light and shadow to make his paintings more exciting. He often made the people and objects in his pictures seem to burst out of the frame. In the one above, Jesus (in the middle) has just surprised his companions. The hand of one and the elbow of another seem to come out of the picture at you.

Classical landscapes

Two French artists, Claude Lorraine and Nicolas Poussin, spent most of their working lives in Rome. Many of their paintings show the hills and plains around Rome. This type of painting is known as a "classical landscape". The figures are tiny, Roman ruins are often included, and the colours are soft greens, blues and browns.

The centre of Baroque art was Rome. Artists from all over Europe came to find out about the latest styles and fashions, and to study the great works of Ancient Rome and the High Renaissance. Many, like Caravaggio, Carracci, Claude and Poussin, made their homes there.

A busy studio master

Grid to help assistants transfer ideas from Rubens' sketches on to canvas.

Rubens brought the fashion of using huge canvases with him from Italy!

The Flemish painter, Peter Paul Rubens, worked in Italy as a young man. He learnt a great deal there. When he returned to Flanders his work was in such demand that he employed other artists to work in his studio and had teams of pupils and assistants. Often he did very little of a painting himself, but supervised each stage of the work.

Rubens was often used as a diplomat by his patrons, who included the rulers of France, Spain, England and Flanders. Here he presents Charles I of England with a painting from the King of Spain, who wanted peace with England.

At the Spanish court

Many of Rubens' paintings are on big canvases and are full of life. He developed a very dramatic, free way of painting, using big, energetic figures. This painting is called "The Battle of the Amazons".

In Spain, the most famous painter of this time was Diego Velazquez. He worked at court and painted many portraits of the king and his family. This one is of the young princess Margarita and Velazquez in his studio.

The Great Century of Dutch Painting

Holland became an independent, Protestant country during the 17th century. Before this it had been ruled by Spain as the northern part of Spanish Netherlands. The new Dutch Republic quickly became a rich and powerful trading nation.

Paintings were immensely popular in 17th century Holland. The demand was so great that many artists had to specialize in doing a particular type of painting, in order to reach a higher standard.

In Roman Catholic countries the Church had always bought a lot of paintings, but Protestants did not approve of religious paintings and Dutch churches were kept very plain.

The new capital city, Amsterdam, became a bustling centre of trade. The merchants who profited from this trade wanted to buy paintings of themselves and their interests.

Popular subjects for painters

Dutch merchants loved to have their portraits painted, either by themselves or in groups. Some of the best-known of these portraits are by the artist, Frans Hals.

Holland also had a prosperous farming community and another popular subject for painters was domestic animals such as cows, sheep and poultry.

Pictures of everyday scenes, like this one, are known as "genre" paintings. Dutch ones show tidy, comfortable rooms in private houses.

Some Dutch painters specialized in pictures of carefully arranged objects, like fruit, flowers, jugs and dishes. These are called "still-life" paintings.

Landscape artists painted views of the flat Dutch countryside, dotted with trees, windmills and churches. They became very skilled at painting large areas of sky.

Holland's wealth was founded on her sea trade, so it was natural that pictures of ships and the sea would be popular. These also showed great expanses of sky.

A Dutch market

Famous artists

AD1581/1666	Frans Hals
AD1606/1669	Rembrandt van Rijn
AD1626/1679	Jan Steen
AD1628/1682	Jacob van Ruisdael
AD1629/1684	Pieter de Hooch
AD1632/1675	Johannes Vermeer

Many artists painted pictures before they had found people to buy them. Before this nearly all pictures were specially ordered by a buyer. Artists sold their paintings at markets and fairs. There was strong competition and it was hard to make a living. Many painters had to do other jobs besides painting.

A number of people started making a living as picture dealers. They bought pictures from artists and sold them at a profit. The artist Vermeer was himself an art dealer.

Rembrandt

Rembrandt is the most famous of all Dutch painters. This is one of over 70 portraits that he did of himself throughout his life. It shows him as a young man.

Rembrandt was a great collector. He bought old-fashioned costumes, armour and weapons at auctions and kept them in his studio so he could paint them into his pictures.

In the early part of his career Rembrandt was a highly successful portrait painter. His most famous painting, "The Nightwatch", is a group portrait of a company of guardsmen in Amsterdam. It is not a formal painting, but even included dogs and children. Each person posed separately for this painting and the figures look quite relaxed.
Later, Rembrandt started to paint, not to please wealthy clients, but just to please himself. He painted stories from the Bible and from ancient history, but he could not always sell them. Despite this, he was extravagant. He spent far more money than he earned and got into debt. His wife and son died and his last years were spent in poverty and loneliness, but he continued to paint.

Rococo and Neoclassical Painting

In the early 18th century, Paris took the place of Rome as the centre of the arts. There a new style called Rococo* developed. Also at this time, excavations at and near Pompeii in Italy, brought to light more classical works of art. This stimulated a new interest in the Ancient World and gave rise to the Neoclassical (new classical) style.

These two styles—Rococo, on this page, and Neoclassical on the facing page—are in strong contrast to each other.

After the death of King Louis XIV in AD1715, French noblemen moved from his grand place at Versailles back to Paris. There they built elegant town houses, which they decorated in the new Rococo style. This room, with its large windows and mirrors, intricate carvings and delicate colours, is typical of this style.

Rococo paintings are usually of cheerful subjects, like well-fed, well-dressed people, enjoying picnics and parties out of doors. They are light and colourful and show the sort of lives French aristocrats wanted to live. This fairyland, where everything is pleasant and peaceful, contrasted strongly with the poverty-stricken lives led by most ordinary people. The most famous painter of this kind of picture was Jean-Antoine Watteau.

In this famous painting by Jean-Honoré Fragonard, the girl on the swing kicks off her shoes while the young man blushes at the glimpse he gets of her legs.

Exhibitions

In the 18th century so many people became interested in art that many societies for the exhibition of paintings were formed. Later some of these became public galleries.

Collectors

Rich connoisseurs built up private collections. They were visited by artists and gentlemen doing the "Grand Tour" of Europe, as part of their education.

*This comes from the French word *rocaille*, which means "rock-work".

◀This room is in the Neoclassical style. Neoclassical architecture, interior design and painting is very plain and simple if you compare it with Rococo.

▼ Artists painted in the style they thought the Ancient Romans would have used and often chose classical subjects. Jacques-Louis David, a Frenchman who had visited Rome, was the most famous Neoclassical painter. The picture below, called "The Oath of the Horatii", shows three young men swearing to fight to the death with the enemies of Rome.

Most English patrons only wanted to buy portraits, but some English artists were able to combine these with other subjects they found more interesting. Thomas Gainsborough often set his figures in light, feathery landscapes.

Sir Joshua Reynolds sometimes dressed his subjects as characters from ancient history and myths.

Academies

Academies were founded in most European capital cities. They held exhibitions and ran schools of painting, which taught strict rules about how to paint properly.

Famous artists

Neoclassical

AD1748/1825   Jacques-Louis David

England

AD1697/1764   William Hogarth
AD1723/1792   Sir Joshua Reynolds
AD1727/1788   Thomas Gainsborough

Rococo

AD1684/1721   Jean-Antoine Watteau
AD1703/1770   François Boucher
AD1732/1806   Jean-Honoré Fragonard

William Hogarth did series of paintings which tell stories. Here a young couple are forced to marry by their greedy fathers. Five scenes later the story ends in disaster.

Romantics and Realists

In the early 19th century a new way of thinking gave rise to a style in painting, literature and music, which is called Romantic.

Romantic artists thought that showing feelings and emotions was more important than anything else. They were inspired by the idea of liberty and by anything mysterious, exciting or exotic and they often looked to history and nature for their subjects. They tended to use strong colours and dramatic effects in their paintings. This type of painting was very different from the Neoclassical style, which many painters still followed and which was taught in the academies.

Another style of painting, which arose at this time, was Realism. Realist painters were reacting against the use of imaginary and idealized subjects. They wanted to paint the world exactly as they saw it, so they chose poor people in everyday situations as their subjects.

Many painters gained their inspiration from writers. The poet, Lord Byron, shown above was one of the great romantic heroes of this age.

This "Mounted Officer of the Guard" is much more than a portrait. Filled with excitement and violent energy, it shows the life of one of Napoleon's soldiers, probably not as it actually was but as the artist, Théodore Géricault, liked to imagine it to be. Géricault loved drama and heroic deeds. He painted this picture when he was 21. He was soon to become a leading figure among French Romantic painters.

The most famous Romantic painter, Eugène Delacroix, loved exotic subjects. "The Death of Sardanapalus", which you can see above, was inspired by the story of the luxury-loving king of Ancient Assyria.

The Spaniard, Francisco de Goya, produced many paintings that show his hatred of the war he saw around him in Spain. Here, he shows Napoleon's troops executing citizens of Madrid.

Nature and Romantic painters

Landscape painting played an important part in the Romantic movement. A favourite theme was to show the power of nature

Towering mountains, storms and rough seas make men seem weak and defenceless.

John Constable's paintings give a realistic view of the English countryside. Most of them are of places in

Suffolk, where he grew up. "The Haywain", (above), is probably his most famous painting.

This painting of a train, by the English painter, Turner, is called "Rain, Steam, Speed". Turner tried to convey a feeling of being

present at a scene, rather than showing what it actually looked like. He did many watercolours as well as oil paintings.

Famous artists

Romantics

AD1746/1828	Francisco de Goya
AD1775/1851	Joseph Mallord William Turner
AD1776/1837	John Constable
AD1791/1824	Théodore Géricault
AD1798/1863	Eugène Delacroix

Realists

AD1819/1877	Gustave Courbet

Watercolours

Watercolours had been used earlier but they became especially popular in England at this time. The paint is diluted with water so that light from the paper shows through.

Painting poor people

Some French artists felt that it was time to stop painting from imagination. They observed and painted

peasants and labourers—people whose lives were hard and unromantic and became known as "Realists".

"The Stonebreakers" by Gustave Courbet caused an uproar when it was first shown. Critics felt that this

was an unworthy subject (It was destroyed during World War II and only photographs of it survive).

Impressionists and Post-Impressionists

The group of painters known as the Impressionists came together as students in Paris during the 1860s. The movement was at its height during the 1870s and continued into the 1880s. The Impressionists were more interested in conveying atmosphere, through their use of light and colour, than in the subject matter of their paintings. The period that followed this involved a variety of different styles, which all come under the description of Post-Impressionist. This just means "after the Impressionists".

1

This painting may not seem very shocking today, but in 1863, when it was painted, it caused a scandal. People said it was rude and badly painted.

It was painted by Edouard Manet. People were so shocked by his paintings that he was not allowed to show them in the "Salons" (the official exhibitions of the French Royal Academy).

2

Manet was not the only artist painting in this new style. A group of them decided to hold their own exhibition. One of the paintings on display was "Impression: Sunrise" (shown above) by Claude Monet. One art critic called the group "Impressionists" because of this painting. He was being rude, but soon they adopted the name for themselves.

Painting out of doors

The Impressionists were interested in light. They painted mainly in the open air and avoided using black, which you rarely see in nature; their shadows are made up of many colours.

Claude Monet painted mainly outside. Sometimes he painted the same place at different times of the day or year to show the effects of changing light on the same scene.

Café life

Many Impressionist paintings show Paris, or places nearby. Some show everyday scenes of people enjoying themselves. Life in the cafés was a favourite subject.

Famous artists

Impressionists

AD1830/1903	Camille Pissaro
AD1832/1883	Edouard Manet
AD1834/1917	Edgar Degas
AD1839/1899	Alfred Sisley
AD1840/1926	Claude Monet
AD1841/1919	Pierre-Auguste Renoir

Post-Impressionists

AD1839/1906	Paul Cézanne
AD1848/1903	Paul Gauguin
AD1853/1890	Vincent van Gogh
AD1859/1891	Georges Seurat
AD1864/1901	Henri de Toulouse-Lautrec

Photographs and painting

Japanese prints

The invention of photography had a great influence on painting. Many people felt that now that a machine could produce accurate pictures of the real world, there was no point in painters doing the same thing.

When portable cameras were invented, photographs, taken from odd angles, could capture, unposed actions, like someone doing up their shoe. Painters like Edgar Degas started painting this type of scene.

During the later 19th century, many Japanese prints were sent to Europe as wrapping paper for other goods. This totally different style of art made a deep impression on many painters.

After the Impressionists

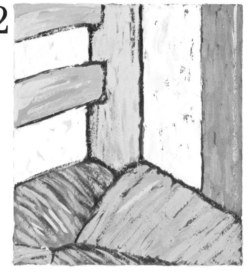

After moving to Paris in 1886, the Dutch painter, Vincent van Gogh, was strongly influenced by both Impressionist paintings and by the Japanese prints he saw there.

He painted everyday subjects in brilliant colours, which he used so thickly that they look as though they have been squeezed straight out of a tube onto the canvas.

Paul Cézanne used the Impressionists' discoveries about light and colour, but painted more solid objects. He often changed their shape, to make the picture as a whole look right.

To paint this picture, "The Lady with the Powder Puff", Georges Seurat used a method called pointillism (using lots of small dots).

He studied the science of colour and realized that if you paint lots of small dots next to each other, they mix in your eye.

This painting by Paul Gauguin is of native women on the island of Tahiti in the South Pacific. Gauguin went to Tahiti in search of simple people and a simple life. The paintings he did there are his best works. He used clear outlines and large patches of flat colour, rather like stained glass windows.

Modern Painting

In the 20th century, many artists have stopped painting recognizable objects. They use colours and shapes to express their ideas and feelings. This kind of painting is usually called "Abstract".

Other painters are still concerned with "representing" real objects, but they use new methods and new subjects. On this page you can see different types of Abstract painting, and on the facing page, Representational painting.

1

2

The round blobs are probably the fruit.

The shape of the neck and head of a guitar can be seen on the left of the picture.

The tall black shape looks like the neck of a bottle with a cork in the top.

Notice the guitar strings going across the sound hole in the centre.

The Spanish painter, Pablo Picasso, and his friend Georges Braque, developed a new style of painting. They chose objects, imagined them to be made up of geometric shapes, and painted them as though seen from many different angles. This style of painting is called Cubism. The painting above is called "Fruit Dish, Bottle and Guitar".

One style that grew out of Post-Impressionism was Expressionism. One Expressionist group worked in Paris. They liked violent colours and often changed the shape of the things they painted. Because of this they became known as the "Fauves" (wild beasts). This picture is by their leader, Henri Matisse. It shows his friend, the artist, André Derain.

3

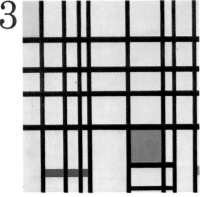

Action Painting

Some artists took the idea of painting in geometric shapes a stage further than the Cubists had done. Piet Mondrian used only straight lines and primary colours.

In the 1940s New York became an important centre for painters. One group, the Action Painters, felt that the way an artist paints is just as important as the picture he creates.

The artist, Jackson Pollock, made his pictures by dribbling paint onto huge canvases laid out on the floor. Others painted large canvases in a single colour.

Painting dreams and fantasies

In the 1920s a style of art called Surrealism appeared. Surrealists painted objects realistically, but combined them in an unusual or nonsensical way. They felt that such odd combinations would stir up ideas and feelings in the backs of people's minds. These paintings often have a dream-like quality. This one by René Magritte is called "Time Transfixed".

Using photographs

The artist David Hockney used small drawings and many black and white and coloured photographs to help him paint this couple in their home.

In paintings like this he gives a realistic record of people and places he knows. This is one of a series of double portraits of his friends.

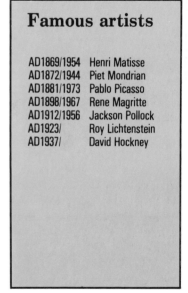

Famous artists

AD1869/1954	Henri Matisse
AD1872/1944	Piet Mondrian
AD1881/1973	Pablo Picasso
AD1898/1967	Rene Magritte
AD1912/1956	Jackson Pollock
AD1923/	Roy Lichtenstein
AD1937/	David Hockney

A very recent development is to project photographs on to canvas and then copy them exactly. Funnily enough, paintings like this, often have a beauty that was not in the photograph.

Pop Art

Since World War II, there has been a move to make art deal with the ordinary world, by painting things that are common in city life. This is called Pop Art.

This painting by Roy Lichtenstein is based on a comic strip. Artists working in this style do not copy directly, but make many changes in size, shape and colour to get the result they want. They seem to want us to look at and enjoy the world around us in a new, fresh way.

Painting in India

In India, religion has always played an important part in the lives of the people and much of its great art has been produced in the service of religion.

The Hindu religion grew up with the beginning of civilisation in India. Buddhism began in about 600BC, and spread to other countries in the East. Islam, the religion of the Muslims, was brought to India from the Middle East, by Muslim warriors. The most famous Muslim invaders were the Moguls, who, in the 16th century, set up an empire in northern India.

Buddhist painting

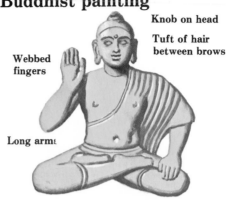

When the Buddha (Prince Gautama, who founded Buddhism) is represented in sculptures or paintings, he always has certain key features, as shown above.

The row of Buddhas, shown above, is in a cave at Ajanta, a Buddhist holy place. Some of the oldest paintings in India are in caves cut into the rocks.

Paintings for Muslim rulers

Some of the finest Indian paintings are the book illustrations produced at the court of the Mogul emperors. The Moguls were immensely rich and great patrons of the arts. Miniature paintings, like the one above, were done in brilliant colours and show great detail. A painting was often produced by a team of artists working together.

The Moguls brought the art of painting miniatures with them from Persia. Persian miniatures, like the one above are more decorative than Mogul ones.

Mogul paintings show scenes from life in the palaces of the princes and emperors, and portraits of the rulers and their families, rather than religious scenes.

Mogul painting had a great influence throughout India. Hindu painters began to use this style to paint religious scenes. The Hindu god, Krishna, usually shown with blue skin, was a favourite subject.

28

Painting in the Far East

As in other parts of the world, painting in the Far East was strongly influenced by religious beliefs, particularly Buddhism and Taoism. Painters aimed at simplicity and stillness in their pictures. The oldest Chinese paintings that survive were painted nearly 2,000 years ago.

For the Chinese, calligraphy (the art of handwriting) was as important an art as painting. A piece of calligraphy was often hung on a wall like a painting, and many paintings have writing on them.

Paintings were often done on scrolls. These could be either hanging scrolls or hand scrolls. Hand scrolls could be up to 30m long. They were kept on rollers and unrolled and viewed section by section.

Painters' materials

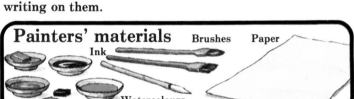

Chinese artists used either ink or watercolours, which they applied with soft brushes with bamboo handles. They painted on either silk or paper.

Chinese artists painted a wide range of subjects, but many of their best paintings are landscapes, like the one above. They painted with incredible speed, but they thought a great deal about the painting before they began, and knew exactly what they were going to do. Once they had begun they could not make any changes.

Japan

In Japan coloured prints, made by using carved blocks of wood, became very popular in the 18th and 19th centuries. Many of the best artists were employed by the publishers of these prints. Their designs were first done on paper, then cut into woodblocks by engravers and printed in their hundreds. They often showed scenes from everyday life, like the fishing scene on the right.

Primitive Art

The term, Primitive Art, is used to describe the art of peoples who have not been influenced by the great centres of civilisation. This includes paintings done by the Eskimos, the Indians of North and South America, Africans and the Aborigines of Australia.

Buffalo hide painted by North American Indians.

Body painting by Indians near the River Amazon, South America.

Painted totem pole by Eskimos in Canada.

Painted mask from Sri Lanka.

Bark painting by Australian Aborigines.

Painted African mask.

Rock painting by African tribes in the Sahara Desert.

Primitive Art, though very different from the art of the developed world, is not necessarily backward. Much of it is extremely sophisticated and skilfully produced. Like the cave paintings done in the Old Stone Age, it often has a magical or superstitious purpose. In the 20th century the art of these isolated peoples has exercised a great influence on many artists in Europe and America.

Paul Gauguin was one of the first European artists to look to the art of isolated peoples for inspiration and ideas. He went to live on the island of Tahiti in the South Pacific.

Some 20th century artists, like Picasso, became excited when they discovered African masks. Primitive carving and sculpture has influenced them more than primitive painting.

Some painters in the developed countries of the world, produce what are known as Primitive paintings. They, like the primitive peoples, are isolated—they are not influenced by traditional styles. Their paintings are very individual but all are simplified. The French artist Henri Rousseau (AD1844/1910), seen above, is a famous example of a Primitive painter.

Acknowledgements

Page 3: Copy of an Egyptian wall painting from the tomb of Menne at Thebes, showing the assessment of crops. Reproduced by permission of the Trustees of the British Museum.

Page 4: *Toreador,* Cretan wall painting from the Palace at Knossos. Heraklion Museum. Photo: Scala.

Page 6: Illuminated pages from the Lindisfarne Gospel. Cotton MS Nero D.iv, fol. 26v and 29. Reproduced by permission of the British Library.

Page 7: *The Lamentation over Christ* by Giotto. Arena Chapel, Padua. Photo: Scala.

Page 8: (top right) *The Tribute Money* by Masaccio. Brancacci Chapel, Santa Maria del Carmine, Florence. Photo: Scala. (bottom right) *Venus and Mars* by Botticelli. National Gallery, London.

Page 10: (left) *The Marriage of Giovanni Arnolfini and Giovanna Cenami* by van Eyck. National Gallery, London. (right) *Hell* by Bosch. Prado, Madrid. Photo: Scala.

Page 11: (centre right) *Anne of Cleves* by Holbein the Younger. Louvre, Paris. Photo: Cooper-Bridgeman Library. (botton left) *Children's Games* by Breugel. Kunsthistorisches Museum, Vienna. Photo: Cooper-Bridgeman Library.

Page 12: (left) *Portrait of Mona Lisa* by Leonardo. Louvre, Paris. Photo: Scala. (right) *Cartoon: The Virgin and Child with St Anne and St John the Baptist* by Leonardo. National Gallery, London.

Page 13: (right) *The School of Athens* by Raphael. Vatican. Photo: Scala. (left) *The Creation of Adam* by Michelangelo. Detail of the ceiling of the Sistine Chapel, Vatican. Photo: Scala.

Page 14: *Madonna of the Long Neck* by Parmigianino. Uffizi Gallery, Florence. Photo: Scala.

Page 15: *The Emperor Charles V* by Titian. Prado, Madrid. Photo: Scala.

Page 16: *The Supper at Emmaus* by Caravaggio. National Gallery, London.

Page 17: (left) *Battle of the Amazons* by Rubens. Alte Pinakothek, Munich. Photo: Cooper-Bridgeman Library. (right) *Maids of Honour* by Velazquez. Prado, Madrid. Photo: Scala.

Page 19: *Self-portrait aged 34* by Rembrandt. National Gallery, London.

Page 20: *The Swing* by Fragonard. Reproduced by permission of the Trustees of the Wallace Collection, London.

Page 21: (left) *The Oath of the Horatii* by David. Louvre, Paris. Photo: Cooper-Bridgeman Library. (top right) *The Morning Walk* by Gainsborough. National Gallery, London.

(centre right) *Three Ladies Adorning a Term of Hymen* by Reynolds. Tate Gallery, London. (botton right) *The Marriage Contract (from Marriage à la Mode)* by Hogarth. National gallery, London.

Page 22: (left) *Officer of the Chasseurs Charging* by Géricault. Louvre, Paris. Photo: Musees Nationaux. (centre right) *Death of Sardanapalus* by Delacroix. Louvre, Paris. Photo: Scala. (bottom right) *The Execution of the Rebels on 3rd May 1808* by Goya. Prado, Madrid. Photo: Scala.

Page 23: (centre right) *Rain Steam and Speed—the Great Western Railway* by Turner. National Gallery, London. (top left) *The Haywain* by Constable. National Gallery, London.

Page 24: (left) *The Luncheon Party* by Manet. Louvre, Paris. Photo: Scala. (right) *Impression, Sunrise* by Monet. Louvre, Paris. Photo: Scala. © S.P.A.D.E.M.

Page 25: (centre left) *The Chair and the Pipe* by van Gogh. Tate Gallery, London. (centre right) *Still-life with Plaster-cast* by Cézanne. Courtauld Institute Galleries, London. (bottom left) *A Young Woman Holding a Powder-Puff* by Seurat. Courtauld Institute Galleries, London. (bottom right) *Nevermore* by Gauguin. Courtauld Institute Galleries, London.

Page 26: (left) *Fruit, Dish, Bottle and Guitar* by Picasso. National Gallery, London. © S.P.A.D.E.M.

(right) *André Derain* by Henri Matisse. Tate Gallery, London. © S.P.A.D.E.M. (bottom left) *Composition with Red, Yellow and Blue* by Mondrian. Tate Gallery, London. © S.P.A.D.E.M.

Page 27: (top left) *Time Transfixed* by Magritte. Art Institute of Chicago. © A.D.A.G.P. Photo: John Webb. (top right) *Mr & Mrs Clark and Percy* by Hockney. Tate Gallery, London. © the artist, courtesy Petersburg Press. (bottom right) *Whaam!* by Lichtenstein. Tate Gallery, London.

Page 28: *The Three Younger Sons of Shah Jahan.* Victoria and Albert Museum, Crown Copyright.

Page 29: Landscape painting Photo: Cooper-Bridgeman Library.
Fishing net and Fuji by Kuniyoshi. Colour woodcut. Victoria and Albert Museum, Crown Copyright.

Page 19: *The Night Watch (The Militia Company of Captain Frans Banning Cocq)* by Rembrandt. Rijksmuseum, Amsterdam. Photo: Scala.

Index